The
HOLY
SPIRIT
in YOU

The HOLY SPIRIT *in* YOU

DEREK PRINCE

Whitaker House

Scripture quotations marked (NAS) are from the *New American Standard Bible*, © 1960, 1962, 1968, 1971, 1973, 1975, 1977 by The Lockman Foundation. Used by permission.

Scripture quotations marked (NIV) are from the Holy Bible, *New International Version*, © 1973, 1978, 1984 by the International Bible Society. Used by permission.

THE HOLY SPIRIT IN YOU

Derek Prince Ministries - International
1800 East Associates Lane
Charlotte, NC 28217

ISBN: 0-88368-238-9
Printed in the United States of America
Copyright © 1987 by Derek Prince

Whitaker House
30 Hunt Valley Circle
New Kensington, PA 15068

5 6 7 8 9 10 11 12 13 / 06 05 04 03 02 01 00 99

Contents

Chapter One

Before Pentecost

Through the Scriptures we receive knowledge we could receive in no other way. One of the supremely important revelations of the Bible is the nature of God. The Bible unfolds a mystery that we could know through no other source. The mystery is that God is both one and yet more than one; three persons, yet one God. The three persons revealed in Scripture are the Father, the Son, and the Holy Spirit. This book will deal with the Holy Spirit.

One of the most profound and distinctive revelations of the whole Bible is that of the person and the work of the Holy Spirit. The first thing we must understand is that the Holy Spirit is Himself a person, just as much as the Father and the Son. Because of human parallels, it is comparatively easy for us to realize that God the Father is a person and God the Son is a person, but it is not as easy to realize that the Holy Spirit is a person.

Through the Holy Spirit, God knows everything, there is nothing hidden from God; and through the Holy Spirit, God is present everywhere at the same time. These two characteristics are represented by the theological terms omniscient and omnipresent, respectively. This is unfolded in various passages of Scripture. For instance, in Jeremiah 23:23-24, the Lord says:

> [23]*"Am I only a God nearby,"*
> > *declares the LORD,*
> *"and not a God far away?*
> [24]*Can anyone hide in secret places*
> > *so that I cannot see him?"*
> > *declares the LORD.*
> *"Do not I fill heaven and earth?"*
> > *declares the LORD.*
> > > *(NIV)*

God fills heaven and earth. There is no place where God is not. There is no place where things happen that God does not know about them. This is very beautifully unfolded in the opening verses of Psalm 139:

*¹O LORD, you have searched me
       and you know me.*
*²You know when I sit and when I rise;
       you perceive my thoughts from afar.*
*³You discern my going out and my lying
down;
       you are familiar with all my ways.*
*⁴Before a word is on my tongue
       you know it completely, O LORD.*
*⁵You hem me in—behind and before;
       you have laid your hand upon me.*
*⁶Such knowledge is too wonderful for me,
       too lofty for me to attain.*
*⁷Where can I go from your Spirit?
       Where can I flee from your presence?*
*⁸If I go up to the heavens, you are there;
       if I make my bed in the depths,
       you are there.*
*⁹If I rise on the wings of the dawn,
       if I settle on the far side of the sea,*

---

*[10] even there your hand will guide me,
      your right hand will hold me fast.
[11] If I say, "Surely the darkness will
   hide me
      and the light become night
      around me,"
[12] even the darkness will not be dark to you;
      the night will shine like the day,
      for darkness is as light to you.*

(NIV)

What beautiful language! What a wonderful unfolding of the greatness of the wisdom of God. God's presence permeates the entire universe. There is nowhere that you can go and be hidden from God. No distance can separate you from Him. No darkness can hide you from Him. God is everywhere, throughout the entire universe. He knows all that is happening in every place.

The key that unlocks the secret is in the seventh verse, where the psalmist says: *"Where can I go from your Spirit? Where can I flee from your presence?"* This is a typical example of Hebrew poetry, where the two halves of the verse say essentially the same thing. God's presence throughout the universe is His Holy Spirit. Through the Holy Spirit, God is present everywhere; and through the Holy Spirit, God knows all that is going on in the universe at any time.

The Holy Spirit has been active in the universe from creation onwards. The psalmist tells us about the actual process of creation:

> [6]*By the word of the LORD the heavens were made,*
> *And by the breath of His mouth all their host.*   *(Psalm 33:6 NAS)*

Where the English translation says "*breath,*" the Hebrew says, literally, "spirit." That would change the reading to: "*By the word of the LORD the heavens were made, and by the 'spirit' of His mouth all their host.*" In other words, the two great agents of creation which brought the whole universe into being were the Word of the Lord and the Spirit of the Lord, or the Holy Spirit. If we turn back to the verses at the beginning of the Bible which describe creation, we see this unfolded in greater detail. Genesis 1:2-3 reads:

> *²Now the earth was formless and empty, darkness was over the surface of the deep, and the Spirit of God was hovering over the waters.*
> *³And God said, "Let there be light," and there was light.* (NIV)

The presence of the Spirit of God was there in the formless darkness, in the void, in the waste. The word *"hovering"* suggests a bird. Many times in Scripture, the Holy Spirit is identified as being the heavenly dove. Here we have heaven's dove, the Holy Spirit, hovering over the dark, formless waste of waters.

Verse three says, *"And God said, 'Let there be light,' and there was light."* Here again are the two agents of creation: the

Spirit of God and the Word of God. When they are united, creation takes place. When the Spirit of God and the Word of God are there, then a new thing—in this case, light—is created. Light comes into being, formed by the Spirit and by the Word of God. You can see that the Holy Spirit has been at work in the universe from creation onwards and has always been present everywhere in the universe. In a sense, the Holy Spirit is the active, effective agent of the Godhead.

The Holy Spirit inspired and empowered all the men of God in the Old Testament. The list is too long to give all the names, but we will consider several examples.

The first one is Bezalel, the man who designed and created the ark and all the furniture for the tabernacle of Moses. The Lord is speaking in Exodus 31:2-3:

> *²"See, I have chosen Bezalel son of Uri, the son of Hur, of the tribe of Judah, ³and I have filled him with the Spirit of God, with skill, ability and knowledge in all kinds of crafts..."* (NIV)

It was the Spirit of God filling Bezalel that gave him the ability to produce such outstanding creative workmanship. It always impresses me that he is the first man in Scripture of whom it was said that he was filled with the Spirit of God. The result, in his case, was craftsmanship. That gives a very high value to craftsmanship.

In Deuteronomy 34:9, we read about Joshua:

> *⁹Now Joshua son of Nun was filled with the spirit of wisdom* [that's another way of saying the Spirit of God] *because Moses had laid his hands on him. So the Israelites listened to* [Joshua] *and did what the LORD had commanded Moses.* (NIV)

Joshua was the great military leader who conquered the Promised Land, and he did it because he was filled with the Spirit of God.

In Judges 6:34, we read about Gideon:

> ³⁴*Then the Spirit of the LORD came upon Gideon, and he blew a trumpet, summoning the Abiezrites to follow him.* (NIV)

The Spirit of the Lord came upon Gideon and made him the mighty leader that he was. Before that, he was a timid young man, cowering at the winepress, unable to do anything effective. But he was changed by the Spirit of God coming upon him.

Then we read about David, the great king and psalmist, in 2 Samuel 23:1-2. This is what David says:

> ¹*Now these are the last words of David. David the son of Jesse declares, And the man who was raised on high declares, The anointed of the God of Jacob, And the sweet psalmist of Israel,*

²"The Spirit of the LORD spoke by me, And His word was on my tongue." (NAS)

David gave us those beautiful psalms because, *"The Spirit of LORD spoke by me ...His word was on my tongue."* Notice again, it is the Spirit of God and the Word of God.

In 2 Peter 1:21, Peter sums up the ministry of all the Old Testament prophets when he says:

²¹For prophecy never had its origin in the will of man, but men spoke from God as they were carried along by the Holy Spirit. (NIV)

Every prophet who brought a true message from God never spoke out of his own initiative or from his own thinking, reasoning, or understanding; but he was inspired (prompted or carried along) by the Holy Spirit. That made his message more than human; it became a message from God Himself.

14

As we look at the examples of these and many other men, we come to the conclusion that all the Old Testament men who served God acceptably and effectively did so solely through the power and inspiration of the Holy Spirit. Surely, this is a lesson for us. If they were unable to effectively serve God without the Holy Spirit, neither can we.

Chapter Two

The Holy Spirit in the Life of Jesus

We will now look at the Holy Spirit in the ministry and teaching of Jesus Himself. First, we need to see that John the Baptist, who came specifically to introduce Jesus and prepare the way for His ministry, introduced Him under one particular title, "the Baptizer in the Holy Spirit."

> [11]*"I baptize you with water for repentance. But after me will come one who is more powerful than I, whose sandals I am not fit to carry. He will baptize you with the Holy Spirit and with fire."*
>
> *(Matthew 3:11 NIV)*

Notice the distinction between Jesus and all the men that had come before Him:

"He will baptize you with the Holy Spirit and with fire." This ministry of Jesus as baptizer in the Holy Spirit is mentioned in all four gospels. The Bible attaches particular importance to it.

We find, too, that the Holy Spirit was the sole source of power for the entire ministry of Jesus. Until the Holy Spirit came upon Jesus at the Jordan River after John's baptism, He never preached or performed a miracle. He waited for the Holy Spirit to come upon Him.

In Acts 10:38, Peter, speaking to the crowd of people gathered in the house of Cornelius, described the ministry of Jesus:

> [38]*...God anointed Jesus of Nazareth with the Holy Spirit and power, and...he went around doing good and healing all who were under the power of the devil, because God was with him.* (NIV)

The source and power of the ministry of Jesus on earth was the Holy Spirit. We have pointed out already that God is revealed as a triune God—three persons in one God—Father, Son, and Spirit. In this one verse, all three persons are identified. God the Father anointed Jesus the Son with the Holy Spirit. The result of the total God in action on the level of humanity was healing: *"...he went around doing good and healing all who were under the power of the devil."* This is the secret and the source of the ministry of Jesus.

Even after the resurrection, Jesus still depended on the Holy Spirit. This is a remarkable fact. In Acts 1:1-2, Luke starts with these words:

> *¹In my former book* [the gospel of Luke], *Theophilus, I wrote about all that Jesus began to do and to teach*
> *²until the day he was taken up to heaven, after giving instructions through the Holy Spirit to the apostles he had chosen. (NIV)*

Luke is speaking about the ministry of Jesus during the forty days between His resurrection and ascension. It says that Jesus gave instructions to His apostles through the Holy Spirit. Jesus is our pattern of total dependence upon the Holy Spirit. He relied on the Holy Spirit for the power for His miracles and for His teaching; He did nothing apart from the Holy Spirit. The challenge of the ministry of Jesus is a challenge to us to depend on the Holy Spirit just as He did.

Jesus not only moved in the power of the Holy Spirit throughout His ministry, He also promised that His disciples would receive the same Holy Spirit that had empowered and inspired Him. In John 7:37-39, we read:

> *37On the last and greatest day of the Feast, Jesus stood and said in a loud voice, "If a man is thirsty, let him come to me and drink.*
> *38Whoever believes in me, as the Scripture has said, streams of living water will flow from within him."*

> [39] *By this he meant the Spirit, whom those who believed in him were later to receive. Up to that time the Spirit had not been given, since Jesus had not yet been glorified.* (NIV)

Here is a tremendously dramatic contrast. We are first presented with a thirsty man: *"If any man thirst."* Then, through the incoming and indwelling of the Holy Spirit, this same man who had been thirsty and without sufficiency for himself becomes a channel for *"streams of living water."* He is no longer in need, but a source of supply through the Holy Spirit. For every believer, the Holy Spirit is to be a limitless resource.

The writer of the gospel then goes on to make it clear that, though the promise was given during the earthly ministry of Jesus, it would not be fulfilled until after Jesus had been glorified. He says, *"Up to that time the Spirit had not been given, since Jesus had not yet been glorified."*

The Holy Spirit in You

In John 14:15-18, Jesus says to His disciples:

> [15]*"If you love me, you will obey what I command.*
> [16]*And I will ask the Father, and he will give you another Counselor to be with you forever—*
> [17]*the Spirit of truth* [this is one of the titles of the Holy Spirit]. *The world cannot accept him, because it neither sees him nor knows him. But you know him, for he lives with you and will be in you.*
> [18]*I will not leave you as orphans; I will come to you."* (NIV)

There are some important points we need to notice here. First, Jesus says, *"the Father...will give you another Counselor."* What is the meaning of the word *"another"* in that context? It means that Jesus, as a person, had been with His disciples for three and one-half years. He says, in effect, "Now, as a person I'm going to leave you. But when I go, another person, the Holy Spirit, will come in my place."

Second, He uses a particular word to describe the Holy Spirit which is translated *"Counselor"* in the New International Version. The Greek word is *parakletos,* and the Catholic versions translate it *"Paraclete."* A *paraclete* is "somebody called in alongside to help." Other translations are *"Comforter"* and *"Helper."* Here we have the three related concepts: counselor, comforter, and helper.

Third, Jesus goes on to point out that the Holy Spirit will remain with the disciples forever. Again, there is a contrast with His own relationship to the disciples. He is basically saying, "I've been with you a brief three and one-half years. I'm leaving now, and your hearts are broken. You feel you're going to be left without help. But I'm going to send you another helper, the Holy Spirit, and when He comes, He'll never leave you. He'll be with you forever." Then He says, "I will not leave you as orphans, but I'll come to you." The implication there is that without the Holy Spirit, they would have been left as orphans with no one to care for them, help them, or instruct them. But through the Holy Spirit, full provision has been made for them.

A little further on in the same discourse, Jesus returns to this theme:

> [7]*"But I tell you the truth: It is for your good that I am going away. Unless I go away, the Counselor will not come to you; but if I go, I will send him to you."*
>
> *(John 16:7 NIV)*

Jesus is going, but another person is coming in His place.

In John 16:12-15, Jesus returns once more to this vital message:

> [12]*"I have much more to say to you, more than you can now bear.*
> [13]*But when he, the Spirit of truth, comes, he will guide you into all truth.*
> [Jesus emphasizes the personality of the Holy Spirit by using the personal pronoun "He."]

> *He will not speak on his own; he will speak only what he hears, and he will tell you what is yet to come.*
> *¹⁴He will bring glory to me by taking from what is mine and making it known to you. ¹⁵All that belongs to the Father is mine. That is why I said the Spirit will take from what is mine and make it known to you."*
>   (NIV)

Since that promise was fulfilled, the Holy Spirit is now the personal, resident representative of the Godhead on earth. He is the interpreter, the revelator, and the administrator for the Father and the Son. Jesus says, "He will take from what is Mine and impart it to you." But He adds, *"What is Mine,"* because *"all that belongs to the Father is Mine."* The Holy Spirit, then, is the interpreter, the revelator, and the administrator of all that the Father and the Son have—all is revealed, interpreted, and administered by the Holy Spirit.

Chapter Three

What Happened at Pentecost

Recall that John the Baptist introduced Jesus as the Baptizer in the Holy Spirit. It was his distinctive introduction to Israel. Second, the Holy Spirit was the source of power for the whole ministry and teaching of Jesus; Jesus depended totally on the Holy Spirit. Third, Jesus promised His disciples that when He Himself went back to heaven, He would send the Holy Spirit in His place as His personal representative to be their *paraclete*—counselor, comforter, or helper—"the one called in alongside to help them."

We now want to consider the fulfillment of this promise that Jesus made. In

particular, we will examine the wonderful
new thing that happened when the Holy
Spirit descended on the day of Pentecost.
As with many of the promises of the Bible,
this promise of the Holy Spirit was not
completely realized in a single event; rath-
er, it was fulfilled in phases. The first
phase took place on what we call Easter
Sunday, which was the day of Jesus'
resurrection. In John 20:19-22, we find:

> *¹⁹On the evening of that first day of the
> week, when the disciples were together,
> with the doors locked for fear of the Jews,
> Jesus came and stood among them and
> said, "Peace be with you!"*
> *²⁰After he said this, he showed them his
> hands and his side.*
> [He demonstrated He was the same one
> they had seen crucified.]
> *The disciples were overjoyed when they
> saw the Lord.*
> *²¹Again Jesus said, "Peace be with you! As
> the Father has sent me, I am sending you."*
> *²²And with that he breathed on them and
> said, "Receive the Holy Spirit."*   (NIV)

The twenty-second verse makes an important statement. The Greek word for Spirit, *pneuma,* also means "breath" or "wind." This act of breathing on them was related to the words Jesus spoke, *"...he breathed on them and said, 'Receive the Holy breath'* [Holy Spirit, the breath of God]."

I believe this was one of the most critical and decisive phases in the entire working out of God's purpose of redemption. What happened at this dramatic moment? First, at that moment, those first disciples entered into what I would call New Testament salvation. In Romans 10:9, Paul laid down the basic requirements for salvation:

9...that if you confess with your mouth Jesus as Lord, and believe in your heart that God raised Him from the dead, you shall be saved.   (NAS)

John 20:19-22 was the first moment at which the disciples really believed God raised Jesus from the dead. Up to that time, they could not enter into salvation as it is presented in the New Testament. At that moment, when they confessed Jesus as their Lord and believed that God had raised Him from the dead, they were saved with New Testament salvation.

The second thing that took place was that the disciples were regenerated, or born again. They became new creations. Each passed out of the old creation into the new creation through the inbreathed breath of God. To understand this, we must look back at the description of the original creation of man in Genesis 2:7:

> [7]*And the LORD God formed man from the dust of the ground and breathed into his nostrils the breath of life, and man became a living being* [or a living soul].   *(NIV)*

The first creation of man took place as God breathed the Spirit of Life (the Breath of Life or the Holy Spirit) into that figure of clay that was on the ground. The inbreathed breath of God, the Holy Spirit, transformed that figure of clay into a living soul. The passage in John, however, speaks of the new creation described by Paul in 2 Corinthians 5:17, *"If any man be in Christ, he is a new creation."* There is a direct parallel between the first creation and the new creation.

In the new creation, Jesus is the resurrected Lord and Savior who has conquered sin, death, hell, and Satan. Having done this, He appeared to His disciples and breathed into them the breath of resurrection life. This was a new kind of life, one that had triumphed over all the forces of evil, death, and sin. Through that experience, the disciples passed out of the old order and entered into New Testament salvation, into the new creation in Christ, through the resurrection breath of life received from Jesus.

However, it is important to understand that even after this Easter Sunday experience, the total fulfillment of the promise of the Holy Spirit had not yet come. After the resurrection Jesus said to the disciples in Luke 24:49:

> [49]*"...behold, I am sending forth the promise of My Father upon you; but you are to stay in the city* [Jerusalem] *until you are clothed with power from on high."* (NAS)

Even more explicitly, shortly before His ascension into heaven and nearly forty days after Resurrection Sunday, Jesus said to them:

> [5]*"For John baptized with water, but in a few days you will be baptized with the Holy Spirit."* (Acts 1:5 NIV)

By this we see that Resurrection Sunday was not the total fulfillment of the promise. Almost all theologians and commentators on Scripture agree that the final and complete fulfillment took place on the day of Pentecost which is described in Acts 2:1-4:

What Happened at Pentecost

¹When the day of Pentecost came, they were all together in one place.
²Suddenly a sound like the blowing of a violent wind came from heaven and filled the whole house where they were sitting.
³They saw what seemed to be tongues of fire that separated and came to rest on each of them.
⁴All of them were filled with the Holy Spirit and began to speak in other tongues as the Spirit enabled them. (NIV)

Pentecost was the actual manifestation and fulfillment of the promise. The Holy Spirit descended from heaven, in person, in the form of a mighty wind, filled each one of them individually, and gave each one a new and supernatural utterance in a language they had never learned.

At the end of this second chapter of Acts, Peter gives a theological explanation of what had taken place:

³²"God has raised this Jesus to life, and we are all witnesses of the fact.

> [33]*Exalted to the right hand of God, he has received from the Father the promised Holy Spirit and has poured out what you now see and hear."* (Acts 2:32-33 NIV)

Again, all three persons of the Godhead are in this verse. Jesus the Son receives the Holy Spirit from the Father and pours out the Holy Spirit on the waiting disciples in the Upper Room in Jerusalem. At that point, the final fulfillment of the promise of the coming of the Holy Spirit took place. The Holy Spirit Himself was released from heaven by the Father and the Son together and descended upon the waiting disciples in the Upper Room in Jerusalem.

Notice that at this point, Jesus was not merely resurrected, but He was also exalted and glorified. Remember, too, that in John 7:39, the writer of the gospel had pointed out that the promise of the Holy Spirit could not be fulfilled until Jesus had been glorified.

We are confronted with two dramatic, wonderful Sundays. The first is Easter Sunday, where we have the resurrected Christ and the inbreathed Spirit. The second is Pentecost Sunday, where we have the glorified Christ and the outpoured Spirit. Remember, each are patterns for all believers, even today.

Easter Sunday	The Resurrected Christ	The Inbreathed Spirit
Pentecost Sunday	The Glorified Christ	The Outpoured Spirit

We will now summarize the permanent significance of the events we have just examined. On the day of Pentecost, the Holy Spirit came down to earth as a person. He is now the resident, personal representative of the Godhead on earth. It seems to be a law (which I cannot explain) that only one person of the Godhead can be resident on earth at any one given time. For some years, it was Jesus the Son. But when Jesus was leaving to return to heaven, He promised that another person would come in His place who would stay with us forever, not just for a few brief years. That promise was fulfilled on the day of Pentecost. Jesus the Son, as a person, had gone back to the Father in heaven. Then, from the Father and the Son together, the Holy Spirit came to take the place of Jesus.

Where does the Holy Spirit now live? There are two answers. First, He lives in the church, the corporate body of Christ. Paul asks the Corinthian believers:

> [16]*Don't you know that you yourselves are God's temple and that God's Spirit lives in you?* *(1 Corinthians 3:16 NIV)*

Paul is talking here about the corporate temple of the Holy Spirit.

Second, in 1 Corinthians 6:19, Paul says something even more dramatic. He reveals that not only is the corporate body of Christ the dwelling place of the Holy Spirit, but it is God's purpose that the body of each believer also be the dwelling place of the Holy Spirit.

> *[19]Do you not know that your body is a temple of the Holy Spirit, who is in you, whom you have received from God?* (NIV)

That is one of the most breathtaking statements found anywhere in the Bible! If we are believers in Jesus Christ, our physical bodies are to be the dwelling place of God the Holy Spirit.

Chapter Four

Our Indwelling Helper

What does it mean for us, practically, that the Holy Spirit has come to be our *paraclete*? We will begin by looking again at the passage in John 14:16-18 where Jesus gave this specific promise:

> *16"And I will ask the Father, and he will give you another Counselor [paraclete] to be with you forever—*
> *17the Spirit of truth. The world cannot accept him, because it neither sees him nor knows him. But you know him, for he lives with you and will be in you.*
> [You can see that this a promise only for believers, not for the world.]
> *18I will not leave you as orphans; I will come to you."* (NIV)

The word *paraclete*, derived from a Greek source, was simply transliterated into English. It literally means "someone who is called in alongside to help." A *paraclete* is someone who can do something for you that you cannot do for yourself. The same Greek word is used in 1 John 2:1:

> ¹*My little children, I am writing these things to you that you may not sin. And if anyone sins, we have an Advocate with the Father, Jesus Christ the righteous.* (NAS)

The word translated here as *"Advocate"* is the source word for *paraclete*. Our English word "advocate" is derived from Latin: *ad*, "to"; and *vocata*, "called"—"somebody called to or in." In almost all languages derived from Latin, the word "advocate" is the word for a lawyer. It means someone who speaks in our defense. We all know the role of an advocate, attorney, or lawyer in contemporary culture.

Scripture unfolds the beautiful truth that we have two advocates. On earth, the

Holy Spirit pleads our cause. The things
we cannot say right, He says for us; the
things we do not understand, He interprets
for us. In heaven, Jesus is our advocate
with the Father; He pleads our cause. Just
think, we have the two greatest advocates
in the universe. We have Jesus Christ, the
Son, at the Father's right hand, and we
have the Holy Spirit on earth. With two
such advocates or attorneys, how could we
ever lose the case?

Let me go on and amplify what Jesus
said about this advocate, who is our *paraclete*—our attorney, comforter, counselor,
and helper. I will comment on some of the
things that Jesus said in John 14:16-18,
cited earlier.

*"The Father will give you another
Counselor."* You must understand the
importance of that word *"another,"* as it
indicates a person. Jesus said, "I'm a
person. I'm going away. When I go, another person will come to be your helper. I've

been your helper while I was here, but now I'm leaving. You're not going to be left without a helper, though. There'll be another helper that will come."

"He will stay with you forever." Jesus says, "I've been with you three and one-half years. I'm leaving you, but don't be heartbroken because there is someone else coming in My place, and He'll never leave you. He'll be with you forever."

"He lives with you and will be in you." There is importance in the phrase *"in you."* This advocate or comforter is going to live in us. We will be His resident address.

"I will not leave you orphans." By implication, if He had gone away and made no provision for them, the disciples would have been left like orphans, without anybody to care for them, help them, or explain things to them.

"I will come to you." This is very important. Christ comes back to His disciples in the Holy Spirit. While He was on earth in His body, Jesus could only be in one place at one time. He could only talk to Peter, John, or Mary Magdalene one at a time, but He could not talk to all three of them, in different conversations, at the same time. He was limited by time and space. Now, when He comes back to His people in the Holy Spirit, He is free from the limitations of time and space. He can be in Australia, talking to a child of God in need there; He can be in the United States anointing a preacher; He can be somewhere in the deserts or the jungles of Africa, strengthening or healing a missionary. He is not limited. He has come back, but no longer subject to the limitations of time or space.

I want to dwell just a little further on this theme of the exchange of persons—one person going, another person coming. In John 16:5-7, Jesus says:

⁵*"Now I am going to him who sent me* [the Father], *yet none of you asks me, 'Where are you going?'*
⁶*Because I have said these things, you are filled with grief.*
⁷*But I tell you the truth: It is for your good that I am going away. Unless I go away, the Counselor will not come to you* [the Comforter]; *but if I go, I will send him to you."*

(NIV)

This is very clear language. "As long as I'm with you, in person, on earth," Jesus says, "the Holy Spirit has to stay in heaven, as a person. But if I go away as a person, then in My place I'll send another person, the Holy Spirit." It is an exchange of divine persons. For a while the Son as a person was on earth, then He went back to heaven with His ministry complete. In His place the Holy Spirit (another divine person) came to complete the ministry that Jesus had begun.

Jesus said it is for our good that He was going away. The King James Version says, *"It is expedient for you."* This is an amazing statement. We are better off with Jesus in heaven and the Holy Spirit on earth than we would be with Jesus on earth and the Holy Spirit in heaven. Few people realize that. Christians are always saying, "If only I could have lived in the days when Jesus was on earth." But Jesus says, "You're better off now. When I'm in heaven and the Holy Spirit is on earth, you will have more then than you have now."

Let me interpret this in the light of the experience of the first disciples themselves. Notice what happened immediately after the Holy Spirit came. There were three immediate results:

First, they understood the plan of God and the ministry of Jesus far better than they had ever understood it while Jesus was on earth. It is a remarkable fact they had been very slow and limited in their understanding, but the moment the Holy Spirit came, they had a totally different comprehension of the ministry and the message of Jesus.

Second, they became extremely bold. Even after the resurrection, they still hid away behind locked doors for fear of the Jews. They were not willing to stand up to preach and proclaim the truth, nor were they equipped. The moment the Holy Spirit came, however, that changed. Peter boldly and straightforwardly told the Jewish people in Jerusalem the whole story of Jesus and laid at their door the guilt of His crucifixion.

Third, they had supernatural confirmations. The moment the Holy Spirit came, miracles began to take place. It was just like Jesus being back with them in person, for Jesus said, "When the Holy Spirit comes, I'll come back in Him. I will be with you. I will not leave you as orphans."

Chapter Five

Revelation of God's Word

The Holy Spirit helps us, comforts us, and meets our needs in very specific ways. The first way we will consider is the revelation of God's Word. The Holy Spirit is the revelator and interpreter of the Word of God. In John 14:25-26, Jesus says to His disciples:

> [25]*"All this I have spoken while still with you.*
> [26]*But the Counselor* [the paraclete], *the Holy Spirit, whom the Father will send in my name, will teach you all things and will remind you of everything I have said to you."*
> (NIV)

47

Two functions of the Holy Spirit which are mentioned in verse 26 are important: He is to remind, and He is to teach. He was to remind the disciples of all that Jesus had already taught them. I understand this to mean that the record of the apostles in the New Testament is not subject to the weaknesses of human memory, but it is inspired by the Holy Spirit. The disciples might not accurately have recalled some things, but whatever they needed to remember, the Holy Spirit Himself brought to their remembrance.

However, He did not merely take care of the past, He also took care of the future. He taught them everything they needed to learn. That is also true for us today. He is our present teacher here on earth. Jesus was the great teacher while He was on earth, but now He has handed over the task to the Holy Spirit, His personal representative. Whatever we need to know about the Word of God, the Holy Spirit is here to instruct us.

This placed the disciples on a level with the Old Testament prophets. Concerning the prophets, Peter wrote in 2 Peter 1:21:

> *21For prophecy never had its origin in the will of man, but men spoke from God as they were carried along by the Holy Spirit.* (NIV)

The accuracy and the authority of the Old Testament prophets was that of the Holy Spirit Himself. He was responsible for what they said as He rested upon them. He inspired them and carried them along. But this is also true of the writings of the New Testament. Jesus made sure that the Holy Spirit would remind the disciples of all that He said and would teach them all that they still needed to know. The Holy Spirit is the true author of all Scripture, both Old and New Testaments. Paul states this very clearly in 2 Timothy 3:16:

> *16All Scripture is God-breathed and is useful for teaching, rebuking, correcting and training in righteousness.* (NIV)

Another translation uses the word *"inspired,"* but either *"inspired"* or *"God-breathed"* both indicate the activity of the Holy Spirit. The Holy Spirit is the one who breathed all Scripture through the human channels by which Scripture came.

God's perfect provision for us causes my heart to rejoice. The Holy Spirit was the author of Scripture, and He is also our personal teacher of Scripture. Thus, the author Himself becomes the interpreter of the Book. Who could ever interpret a book better for you than the one who wrote it? I have written over twenty books myself. Sometimes I hear other people interpret my books, and often they do a good job, but I always think, "Well, you missed that," or, "You didn't get that quite right." In this situation, the Holy Spirit, who is the author of Scripture, is also the interpreter. He misses nothing; He has it all right. If we can listen to Him and receive from Him, we will know what the Scripture really has to say.

The revealing of the Scripture was an immediate result on the day of Pentecost. When the Holy Spirit fell, the unbelieving crowd said, "They're drunk!" But Peter stood up and said:

15"These men are not drunk, as you suppose. It's only nine in the morning!
16No, this is what was spoken by the prophet Joel..." (Acts 2:15-16 NIV)

Up to that time, Peter had no understanding of the prophecy of Joel. In fact, he had a very limited understanding even of the teaching of Jesus. But the moment the Holy Spirit came, the Bible made sense for him in a totally new way because the author was there to interpret.

It is the same with the apostle Paul. He had been persecuting the church and rejecting the claims of Jesus. Acts 9:17 reads:

17Then Ananias went to the house [where Paul was] and entered it. Placing his

hands on Saul [who later became Paul],
he said, "Brother Saul, the Lord—Jesus,
who appeared to you on the road as you
were coming here—has sent me so that you
may see again and be filled with the Holy
Spirit."   *(Acts 9:17 NIV)*

Immediately after that, Paul began to
preach in the synagogues that Jesus was
the Son of God, the very thing he had been
denying. But the moment the Holy Spirit
came in, he had a totally different understanding. It was like the transition from
darkness to light. It was not something
gradual, but almost an instant transforma-
tion because the Holy Spirit, the teacher
and author of Scripture, was in Paul.

When speaking about the Holy Spirit
as the interpreter and the revelator of the
Word of God, we need to bear in mind that
not only is the Bible the Word of God, but
Jesus Himself is called the Word of God. In
John 1:1, we read of Jesus:

> ¹*In the beginning was the Word, and the Word was with God, and the Word was God.* (NIV)

Three times in that verse He is called *"the Word."* John 1:14 states:

> ¹⁴*The Word became flesh and lived for a while among us. We have seen his glory, the glory of the one and only Son, whom came from the Father, full of grace and truth.* (NIV)

The Bible, the Scripture, is the written Word of God, and Jesus is the personal Word of God. Of course, the marvelous thing is they are in total agreement.

Not only does the Holy Spirit reveal and interpret the written Word of God, but He also reveals and interprets the personal Word of God, Jesus. This is what Jesus says about the Holy Spirit:

> ¹²*"I have much more to say to you, more than you can now bear.*

¹³But when he, the Spirit of truth, comes, he will guide you into all truth. He will not speak on his own; he will speak only what he hears, and he will tell you what is yet to come.
¹⁴He will bring glory to me by taking from what is mine and making it known to you.
¹⁵All that belongs to the Father is mine. That is why I said the Spirit will take from what is mine and make it known to you."   *(John 16:12-15 NIV)*

Verse twelve tells us Jesus did not try to say it all because He trusted the Holy Spirit, and He knew the Holy Spirit was coming. Then He explained what the Holy Spirit would do when He came.

The Holy Spirit takes what belongs to Jesus and makes it known to us. He glorifies Jesus for us. He reveals Jesus in His glory, in His totality. Every aspect of the nature, character, and ministry of Jesus is unfolded to us by the Holy Spirit.

It is very interesting to note that once the Holy Spirit descended on the apostles

and the disciples on the day of Pentecost in
Jerusalem, they never had any further
doubts where Jesus was. They knew that
He had arrived in glory at the Father's
right hand. The Holy Spirit had glorified
Jesus to the disciples. He had taken the
things of Christ—in the Scripture, out of
their memories, and out of their contacts
with Jesus—and He had revealed them to
the disciples.

The Holy Spirit reveals and glorifies
Jesus. He also administers the total wealth
of the Father and the Son because all that
the Father has, is given to the Son and all
the Son has, the Holy Spirit administers.
In other words, the total wealth of the
Godhead is administered by the Holy Spirit. It is no wonder we need not be orphans
when He is our administrator and all the
wealth of God is at His disposal.

Chapter Six

Lifted onto a Supernatural Plane

The next main result of the coming of the Holy Spirit is that we are lifted onto a supernatural plane of living. Two very interesting verses in Hebrews describe Christians by a New Testament standard:

> *⁴...those who have once been enlightened, who have tasted the heavenly gift, who have shared in the Holy Spirit,*
> *⁵ who have tasted the goodness of the word of God and the powers of the coming age.*
> *(Hebrews 6:4-5 NIV)*

Here, five things are listed about the New Testament believers:

First, they have been *"enlightened."*

Second, they have *"tasted the heavenly gift"*—which I believe is the gift of eternal life in Jesus.

Third, they have *"shared in the Holy Spirit,"* or been made partakers of the Holy Spirit.

Fourth, they have *"tasted the goodness of the Word of God"*—that is, God's Word has become living and real to them.

Fifth, they have *"tasted the powers of the coming age."*

All Christians believe that in the next age we will function in a totally different way. We will be set free of many of the limitations of our physical bodies, because we will have a different kind of body and a totally different lifestyle. But many Christians do not realize that through the Holy Spirit we can taste a little of this lifestyle right now in this life. We can *"taste...the powers of the coming age."* We can only taste them, not appropriate them in their fullness; but we can come to know a little bit of what the next life is going to be like even during this life.

Paul used a very interesting phrase in this connection. In Ephesians 1:13-14 he is writing to believers:

> *13And you also were included in Christ when you heard the word of truth, the gospel of your salvation. Having believed, you were marked in him with a seal, the promised Holy Spirit,*
> *14who is a deposit guaranteeing our inheritance until the redemption of those who are God's possession—to the praise of his glory.*   *(NIV)*

The word *"deposit"* is a fascinating word. The Holy Spirit is God's deposit in us, right now, for the next age. I have made a study of the word used here. In Greek, it is *arrabon*, which is really a Hebrew word.

Years ago, probably about 1946, when I was living in Jerusalem, I had a very interesting experience which beautifully illustrated for me the meaning of that word *arrabon* or *"deposit."* My first wife and went to the Old City to buy some material to make drapes for our new home. We saw the material that we wanted, inquired about the price (let us say it was $1.00 a yard), and informed the merchant we needed fifty yards. So I told the man, "That's what we want," and he told me the price, $50.00. "Well," I said to him, "I don't have fifty dollars with me right now. Here's ten dollars, that's my deposit. Now the material is mine. You put it to one side. You're not free to sell it to anybody else. I'll come back with the rest of the money, and I'll collect the drapes." Well, that is the word *arrabon*.

The Holy Spirit is the Lord's deposit in us. He makes a down payment of the life of the next age in us right now by giving the Holy Spirit. When we receive that down payment, we are like that drapery fabric. We are set aside, not to be sold to anybody else. It is the guarantee that He is coming back with the rest to complete the purchase. That is why Paul speaks about having a deposit *"until the redemption of those who are God's possession."* We already belong to Him but we have only received the down payment— the full payment is yet to come.

The Holy Spirit is the down payment of our life in God in the next age. This supernatural life extends to every area of our experience.

I want to quote a passage from my book, *The Spirit-filled Believer's Handbook,* which emphasizes this. I wrote as follows:

> If we study the New Testament with an open mind, we are compelled to acknowledge that the whole life and experience of the early Christians was permeated in every part by the supernatural. Supernatural experiences were not

something incidental, or additional; they were an integral part of their whole lives as Christians. Their praying was supernatural; their preaching was supernatural; they were supernaturally guided, supernaturally empowered, supernaturally transported, supernaturally protected.

Remove the supernatural from the book of Acts, and you are left with something that has no meaning or coherence. From the descent of the Holy Spirit in Acts 2, and onwards, it is impossible to find a single chapter in which the record of the supernatural does not play an essential part.

In the account of Paul's ministry in Ephesus, in Acts 19:11, we find a most arresting and thought-provoking expression:

Now God worked extraordinary miracles by the hands of Paul. (NAS)

Consider the implications of that phrase "unusual miracles." The Greek could be translated, somewhat freely, "miracles of a kind that do not happen every day." Miracles were an everyday occurrence in the early church. Normally they would have caused no special surprise or comment. But the miracles granted here in Ephesus through the ministry of Paul were such that even the early church found them worthy of special record.

In how many churches today would we find occasion to use the phrase— "miracles of a kind that do not happen every day"? In how many churches today do miracles ever happen—let alone, happen every day?

One area in which the supernatural was particularly manifested in the lives of the early Christians was in the supernatural direction that they received from the Holy Spirit. In Acts 16, we read about Paul and his companions on his second missionary journey. They were in what we call Asia Minor today, and Scripture says they were:

> *⁶...kept by the Holy Spirit from preaching the word in the province of Asia.*
> *⁷...they tried to enter Bithynia, but the Spirit of Jesus* [or Jesus, through the Holy Spirit] *would not allow them to* [enter Bithynia]. *(Acts 16:6-7 NIV)*

So they tried to go west, and the Holy Spirit would not let them. Then they tried to go northeast, and the Holy Spirit said, "No." Acts 16:8-10 continues:

> *⁸So they passed by Mysia and went down to Troas* [that was northwest].
> *⁹During the night Paul had a vision of a man of Macedonia standing and begging him, "Come over to Macedonia and help us."*
> *¹⁰After Paul had seen the vision, we got ready at once to leave for Macedonia, concluding that God had called us to preach the gospel to them* [in Macedonia].
> *(NIV)*

That is a very significant incident, and it is our example of the supernatural intervention and overruling of the Holy Spirit.

It would have been natural for them in that geographical situation to go either west into Asia or northeast into Bithynia. It was unnatural to pass those two areas, go northwest, and then cross over into the continent of Europe.

However, if we look back over the subsequent history of the church, we see that the continent of Europe played a unique role—first, in preserving the gospel through the Dark Ages; and second, in becoming the main continent for many years to send forth the Word of God to other nations. God had a sovereign purpose that included many centuries ahead. Paul and his companions could never have discovered it by natural reasoning, but through the supernatural direction of the Holy Spirit they walked right into the full purpose of God. All history has been affected by that supernatural guidance of the Holy Spirit in their lives.

That is just a single example out of many of the supernatural interventions of the Holy Spirit in the lives of the early Christians.

Chapter Seven

Help in Prayer

The third vitally important way in which the Holy Spirit helps us is in our prayers. In Romans 8:14 Paul describes our need of the Holy Spirit's guidance to lead the Christian life:

> *14For all who are being led by the Spirit of God, these are sons of God.* (NAS)

In order to become a Christian, you must be born of the Spirit of God. But in order to live like a Christian and come to maturity after you have been born again, you must be led continually by the Spirit of God. The form of the verb that Paul uses there is the continuing present. *"For all who are being* [continually] *led by the Spirit of God, these are sons of God."* They are no longer little babies, but mature sons and daughters.

Further on in Romans, Paul applies this principle of being led by the Holy Spirit particularly to our prayer life. He emphasizes the necessity of the guidance of the Holy Spirit to pray aright.

> [26]*And in the same way the Spirit also helps our weakness; for we do not know how to pray as we should, but the Spirit Himself* [the personality of the Holy Spirit is emphasized] *intercedes for us with groanings too deep for words;*
> [27]*and He who searches the hearts knows what the mind of the Spirit is, because He intercedes for the saints according to the will of God.*   (Romans 8:26-27 NAS)

Paul speaks here about a weakness that we all have. It is not a physical weakness, but a weakness of the mind and understanding. We do not know what to pray for, and we do not know how to pray.

Help in Prayer

I have often challenged congregations by asking people to raise their hands if they **always** knew what to pray for and how to pray for it. Never once has anybody dared to raise his hand on that challenge. I think we are all honest enough to acknowledge that when we want to pray, we often do not know what to pray for. Sometimes, even if we think we know what to pray for, we do not know how to pray for it. Paul calls that *"our weakness."* But he tells us that God sends the Holy Spirit to help us in that weakness, to know what to pray for and to know how to pray for it. In a certain sense, Paul's language suggests that the Holy Spirit moves in and does the praying through us.

The key to effective praying is learning how to be so related to the Holy Spirit that we can submit to the Him. Then we can let Him guide, direct, inspire, and strengthen, and many times actually pray through us.

The New Testament reveals many ways in which the Holy Spirit can help us, a few of which I will now outline.

The first way is referred to in those verses in Romans 8:26-27. Paul says, *"...the Spirit Himself intercedes for us with groanings too deep for words."* I would call that **intercession**, which is one of the high points of the Christian life. Then he speaks about *"groanings to deep for words."* Our finite, limited minds do not have the words to pray what needs to be prayed. So one of the ways the Holy Spirit comes to our help is to pray through us with groanings that cannot be expressed in words.

This is a very sacred experience, a spiritual travail that leads to spiritual birth. Isaiah 66:8 refers to this:

> 8*"As soon as Zion travailed, she also brought forth her sons."* (NAS)

No real spiritual reproduction in the church can occur without spiritual travail in prayer. It is when Zion travails that she brings forth her sons.

Paul confirms this in Galatians 4:19:

¹⁹My dear children, for whom I am again in the pains of childbirth until Christ is formed in you... (NIV)

Paul had preached to those people and they had been converted. But for them to become what they needed to be, Paul recognized that it took more than preaching, it took intercessory prayer. He describes that intercessory prayer as being *"in the pains of childbirth,"* or *"groanings too deep for words."*

A second way in which the Holy Spirit helps us in prayer is that **He illuminates our minds.** He does not actually pray through us in this way, but He shows us in our minds what we need to pray for and

how we need to pray for it. There are two
passages from the epistles that speak about
the work of the Holy Spirit in our minds.
In Romans 12:2, we read:

> ²*And do not be conformed to this world,
> but be transformed by the renewing of your
> mind, that you may prove what the will of
> God is, that which is good and acceptable
> and perfect.* (NAS)

Only a renewed mind can find out
God's will, even in the matter of prayer.
Ephesians 4:23 says:

> ²³*...that you be renewed in the spirit of
> your mind...* (NAS)

The renewing of our minds is done by
the Holy Spirit. When the Holy Spirit
moves in and renews our minds, then we
begin to understand the will of God, and
we begin to know how to pray according to
the will of God. This second way the Holy
Spirit helps us is by renewing our minds,

illuminating them, and revealing to us how to pray.

The third way in which the Holy Spirit helps us is that **He puts the right words in our mouths**, often unexpectedly. Whenever I refer to this, I always think of an incident with my first wife. We were in Denmark, which was her native country, at the end of October. We were leaving the next day to spend the whole month of November in Britain. I am British, so I know that November in Britain is a cold, gloomy, misty, foggy month. As we prayed on the day before we were to leave for Britain, I heard Lydia say, "Give us fine weather all the time we're in Britain!" I almost fell out of the bed where we were sitting and praying.

Afterwards, when I asked her if she knew what she had prayed, Lydia replied, "No, I don't remember!" That was sure proof to me it was the Holy Spirit.

"Well," I said, "you prayed for God to give us fine weather all the time we're in Britain, and you know what Britain is like in November." She just shrugged her shoulders. We spent the whole month of November in Britain, and we had not one cold, miserable, wet day! It was like a good spring.

When we left at the end of November, I said to the people who saw us off at the airport, "Look out, because when we leave the weather's going to change!" Sure enough, it did! That was a prayer that the Holy Spirit put in Lydia's mouth. It was what the Lord wanted her to pray for at that time.

A fourth way the Holy Spirit helps us in prayer is one which is mentioned many times in the New Testament. **He gives us a new, unknown language,** one that the natural mind does not know. Some people today speak about this as a prayer language. Paul says in 1 Corinthians 14:2:

74

²For anyone who speaks in a tongue [an unknown language] *does not speak to men but to God. Indeed, no one understands him; he utters mysteries with his spirit.*

(NIV)

And in verse 4 of that same chapter, Paul says:

⁴He who speaks in a tongue edifies himself...   *(1 Corinthians 14:4 NIV)*

This kind of prayer serves three basic functions:

First, when we pray in an unknown tongue, we are not speaking to men, but to God. To me, that is a tremendous privilege in itself.

Second, we are speaking things our minds do not understand. We are speaking mysteries or sharing God's secrets.

Third, as we do this, we are edifying ourselves, or building ourselves up.

Further on in 1 Corinthians 14:14, Paul says:

14For if I pray in a tongue, my spirit prays, but my mind is unfruitful.   (NIV)

Here is a situation where the Holy Spirit does not illuminate the mind, but He simply gives us a new language and prays through us in that language. We must not use one form of prayer to the exclusion of the other. Paul says very clearly, *"I will pray with my spirit, but I will also pray with my mind"* (verse 15). Both kinds of prayer are possible.

When we let the Holy Spirit in, yield to Him, and let Him work in us according to Scripture, there is a tremendous richness and variety in our prayer life. This is what God wants for each one of us.

Chapter Eight

Life and Health for Our Bodies

The fourth function of the Holy Spirit as *paraclete* is His impartation of supernatural life and health to our physical bodies. Jesus came to give us life, as He declares in John 10:10:

> *10The thief comes only to steal and kill and destroy; I have come that they may have life, and have it to the full.* (NIV)

Two persons are set before us here, and we need to distinguish very clearly between them: the Life-giver, Jesus, and the life-taker, Satan. The devil only comes into our lives to take life. He comes to steal the blessings and the provisions of God; he comes to kill us physically and destroy us eternally. Every one of us needs to realize that if we permit the devil to have any place in our lives, that is what he is going to do—steal, kill, and destroy to the extent we permit him to do so.

On the other hand, Jesus came to do the exact opposite: He came that we may have life and that we might have it to the full. It is important for us to realize that this life Jesus came to give us is administered by the Holy Spirit. We only have His life in the proportion that we allow the Holy Spirit to do His work in us. If we resist or refuse the work of the Holy Spirit, then we cannot experience the fullness of divine life which Jesus came to bring us. We need to understand that it was the Holy Spirit who raised the dead body of Jesus from the tomb. Paul says this in Romans 1:4 about Jesus:

[4]...[Jesus] *through the Spirit of holiness was declared with power to be the Son of God by his resurrection from the dead...*

(NIV)

"The Spirit of holiness" is a Greek translation of the Hebrew phrase for the Holy Spirit. Though Paul was writing in Greek, he was thinking in Hebrew. So when Paul says, *"through the Spirit of holiness,"* it is the same as saying, "through the Holy Spirit, Jesus was manifested or declared to be the Son of God by the power that raised Him from the dead [that is, the power of the Holy Spirit]."

In previous sections I pointed out that, in a certain sense, this was the climax of the redemptive process of God in this age: that God Himself, in the Person of the Holy Spirit, should indwell our physical bodies and make them His temple or His dwelling place. In Romans 8:10-11, Paul says this:

> *10But if Christ is in you, your body is dead because of sin, yet your spirit is alive because of righteousness.*
> *11And if the Spirit of him who raised Jesus from the dead is living in you, he who raised Christ from the dead will also give*

*life to your mortal bodies through his
Spirit, who lives in you.*　　　　(NIV)

The implication of the tenth verse is
that when Christ comes in, when we are
converted and regenerated, an old life ends,
and a new life begins. The old, carnal life is
terminated, and our spirits come alive with
the life of God. Then Paul goes on to say,
in verse eleven, what it means for our
physical bodies. Very clearly, the same
Person, the same power, that raised the
body of Jesus from the tomb is now dwelling in the body of each yielded believer and
is imparting to each mortal body the same
kind of life that He imparted to the mortal
body of Jesus and the same kind of power
that raised Him with an eternal body.

This process of imparting divine life to
our bodies will not be consummated until
the general resurrection from the dead. It
is important to understand that we do not
now have resurrection bodies, but what we
do have is resurrection life in our mortal

bodies. Paul further continues, in several different passages, that resurrection life in our mortal bodies can take care of all the physical needs of our bodies until the time that God separates spirit from body and calls us home.

We must understand how our bodies were formed in the first place because it all relates together. Genesis 2:7 states:

> *⁷And the LORD God formed man from the dust of the ground and breathed into his nostrils the breath* [or the Spirit] *of life, and man became a living being* [or a living soul].   (NIV)

What was it that produced man's physical body? It was the inbreathed Spirit of God that transformed a clay form into a living human being with all the miracles and marvels of a functioning human body. The Holy Spirit originally brought the physical body into being. Logically it follows that He's the one to sustain it. This is so logical, if only Christians can see it.

Divine healing and divine health are logical in the light of Scripture.

For instance, if your watch goes wrong, you do not take your watch to the boot-maker; you take your watch to the watch-maker. Now, apply that same reasoning: if your body goes wrong, where do you take your body? In my opinion, the logical thing to do is to take it to the body-maker, and that is the Holy Spirit.

Here in the United States, we are familiar with the little phrase, "Body by Fisher" on the chassis or body of many of our most common cars. When I look at a fellow Christian, I say, "Body by the Holy Spirit." This is who gave him his body, who sustains his body, and who gives power to his body.

Paul's testimony is impressive. In 2 Corinthians 11:23-25 he says:

²³I have worked much harder, been in prison more frequently, been flogged more severely, and been exposed to death again and again.
²⁴Five times I received from the Jews the forty lashes minus one.
²⁵Three times I was beaten with rods, once I was stoned, three times I was shipwrecked, I spent a night and a day in the open sea... (1 Corinthians 11:23-25 NIV)

It is almost incredible that a man could go through all that and be so active, so healthy, and so courageous. What was the power that sustained Paul in all that? The power of the Holy Spirit. This is the account of the stoning of Paul in Lystra:

¹⁹Then some Jews came from Antioch and Iconium and won the crowd over. They stoned Paul and dragged him outside the city, thinking he was dead.
[And it takes a lot of stones to make a man even appear dead.]
²⁰But after the disciples had gathered around him, he got up and went back into the city. The next day he and Barnabas left for Derbe.   (Acts 14:19-20 NIV)

What a man! I have heard some people suggest that Paul was a walking invalid who went around sick most of the time. My comment on that is, "If Paul was an invalid, God give us a lot more invalids like Paul!"

We have looked briefly at the remarkable record of the physical endurance and resilience of the apostle Paul. We will now look at his secret. What does he say about this? In 2 Corinthians 4:7-12, Paul relates:

> *7But we have this treasure in jars of clay* ["this treasure" is the indwelling Spirit of God] *to show that this all-surpassing power is from God and not from us.*
> *8We are hard pressed on every side, but not crushed; perplexed, but not in despair;*
> *9persecuted, but not abandoned; struck down, but not destroyed.*
> *10We always carry around in our body the death of Jesus, so that the life of Jesus may also be revealed in our body.*
> *11For we who are alive are always being given over to death for Jesus' sake, so that*

> *his life may be revealed in our mortal
> body.*
> *¹²So then, death is at work in us, but life is
> at work in you.* (NIV)

Verses seven and eight tell us we are
not different kinds of persons in ourselves,
but we have a different kind of power in
us. Things that would crush other men
need not crush us because we have a power
in us that makes us resilient.

We find a beautiful contrast in verse
ten. We are to reckon ourselves dead with
Jesus. As we do, then His life is manifested
in our physical bodies. It is very clear that
it is not in the next age, but in this age
that the supernatural, indwelling, resurrection life of Jesus in the Holy Spirit is to be
manifested in our physical bodies.

The last words of verse eleven are
significant: *"...so that his life may be revealed in our mortal body."* This is not just
a secret, indwelling presence that no one
can see; it is a presence that works such

results in our physical bodies that it is evident to everybody. The resurrection life of Jesus is revealed in our mortal bodies.

Verse twelve tells us that when we receive the sentence of death in ourselves and come to the end of our own physical strength and abilities, then a new kind of life works through us to others.

> *16Therefore we do not lose heart, but though our outer man is decaying, yet our inner man is being renewed day by day.*
>   *(2 Corinthians 4:16 NAS)*

The outward man decays, but there is a life in the inner man that is renewed day by day. The inner, supernatural, miraculous life of God takes care of the needs of the outer man for each of us.

Chapter Nine

Outpouring of Divine Love

The greatest and most wonderful of all the blessings the Holy Spirit offers us is the outpouring of God's divine love in our hearts. Romans 5:1-5 says:

> [1]*Therefore, since we have been justified through faith, we have peace with God through our Lord Jesus Christ,*
> [2]*through whom we have gained access by faith into this grace in which we now stand. And we rejoice in the hope of the glory of God.*
> [3]*Not only so, but we also rejoice in our sufferings, because we know that suffering produces perseverance;*
> [4]*perseverance, character; and character, hope.*

⁵And hope does not disappoint us, because God has poured out his love into our hearts by the Holy Spirit, whom he has given us. (Romans 5:1-5 NIV)

The climax comes in the fifth verse: *"And hope does not disappoint us, because God has poured out his love into our hearts by the Holy Spirit, whom he has given us."*

Paul outlines some stages of spiritual progression in those five verses, which I would like to go through very briefly:

The first stage is that we have peace with God.

Second, we have access into God's grace through faith.

Third, we rejoice in hope of God's glory, the hope of something in the future.

Fourth, we rejoice also in sufferings (because of the results sufferings produce in us when we rightly receive them).

Paul then lists three successive results of suffering, rightly endured: the first, perseverance; the second, proven character; and the third, hope.

Then we come to the climax: God's love is poured out in our hearts by the Holy Spirit. Here, the word for *"love"* is the Greek word *agape*, which in the New Testament is normally, but not invariably, restricted to God's own love. Usually, *agape* love is not humanly achievable except by the Holy Spirit. In most cases, we can never produce *agape* in our natural man.

Further in the fifth chapter, Paul defines the nature of *agape*. He explains how it was manifested in God and in Christ:

⁶You see, at just the right time, when we were still powerless, Christ died for the ungodly.

> [7]Very rarely will anyone die for a righteous man, though for a good man someone might possibly dare to die.
> [8]But God demonstrates his own [agape] love for us in this: While we were still sinners, Christ died for us.
>
> *(Romans 5:6-8 NIV)*

When Christ died for us, according to Paul, there were three words that described us: *"powerless," "ungodly,"* and *"sinners."* It is *agape* love which is self-giving and does not lay down any prior conditions. It is not a love that says you must be good, or do this or that. It is freely given out, even to the most undeserving, the most helpless, and the most unworthy.

Now we will trace in the New Testament the various phases in which *agape* love is produced in us. First, it is the product of the new birth. In 1 Peter 1:22-23 we read:

> [22]Now that you have purified yourselves by obeying the truth so that you have sincere

love for your brothers, love one another
deeply, from the heart.
23For you have been born again, not of
perishable seed, but of imperishable,
through the living and enduring word of
God. (NIV)

The possibility of loving with *agape* love originates with the new birth—the new birth of the eternal, incorruptible seed of God's Word which produces in us a new kind of life. *Agape* love is the very nature of that new life. 1 John 4:7-8 says:

7Dear friends, let us love one another, for
love comes from God. Everyone who loves
has been born of God and knows God.
8Whoever does not love does not know God,
because God is love. (NIV)

You can see that this kind of love is the mark of the new birth. A person who has been born again has it; the person who has not been born again cannot have it.

Paul describes the next phase of this process of imparting divine love to us:

⁵And hope does not disappoint us, because God has poured out his love into our hearts by the Holy Spirit, whom he has given us. *(Romans 5:5 NIV)*

After the new birth, in that new nature that is produced by the new birth, the Holy Spirit pours out the totality of God's love into our hearts. We are immersed in love. We are brought in contact with an inexhaustible supply—the total love of God has been poured out into our hearts by the Holy Spirit. I want to emphasize that it is something divine, inexhaustible, and supernatural—something that only the Holy Spirit can do.

Compare what Jesus says in John 7:37-39:

³⁷On the last and greatest day of the Feast, Jesus stood and said in a loud voice, "If a man is thirsty, let him come to me and drink.
³⁸Whoever believes in me, as the Scripture has said, streams of living water will flow from within him."

[39] By this he meant the Spirit, whom those who believed in him were later to receive.
(John 7:37-39 NIV)

You can see the contrast. First, we have a thirsty man who does not have enough for himself. But when the Holy Spirit comes in, that thirsty man becomes a channel for streams of living water. That is the love of God poured out into our hearts. It is not human love; it is not just a portion of God's love. It is the totality of God's love, and we are simply immersed in it. The whole, endless, infinite love of God has a channel to flow through our lives by the Holy Spirit. A thirsty man becomes a channel of streams of living water.

We will now look at the famous love chapter written by Paul and found in 1 Corinthians. At the end of chapter twelve, he says: *"...I show you a still more excellent way."* That *"still more excellent way"* is unfolded in the opening verses of chapter thirteen:

The Holy Spirit in You

> *¹If I speak with the tongues of men and of angels, but do not have love [agape], I have become a noisy gong or a clanging cymbal. ²And if I have the gift of prophecy, and know all mysteries and all knowledge; and if I have all faith, so as to remove mountains, but do not have love, I am nothing. ³And if I give all my possessions to feed the poor, and if deliver my body to be burned, but do not have love, it profits me nothing.* (1 Corinthians 13:1-3 NAS)

It is important to see that all the gifts and manifestations of the Holy Spirit are intended to be channels or instruments of divine love. If we do not use those gifts and make them available to the love of God, we frustrate God's purposes. We may have all the other gifts, but we are simply left like a noisy gong or a clanging cymbal. We are nothing, and we have nothing without divine love.

In verse one Paul says: *"If I speak with the tongues of men and of angels, but do not have love, I have become a noisy gong or a clanging cymbal."* When the Holy

Spirit comes in, He comes into a heart that has been purified by faith and is turned toward God. Later on, it is possible to dry up, miss God's purpose, or misuse what God has made available to us. In that case, it happens as Paul said, *"I have become a noisy gong or a clanging cymbal."* In effect, he says, "I wasn't that way when I received, but through missing the purpose, I have become like that, and I frustrated God's purpose."

Compare that with what Paul says in 1 Timothy 1:5-6:

> *⁵The goal of this command is love, which comes from a pure heart and a good conscience and a sincere faith.*
> *⁶Some have wandered away from these...*
> *(NIV)*

The goal of all Christian ministry is love. The purpose of God for the Christian is the consistent expression of divine love.

I will sum up the three phases in this process of imparting God's love to us:

The first phase is the new birth. When we are born again, we become capable of that kind of love.

The second is the outpouring of the totality of God's love into our hearts by the Holy Spirit who is given to us. The inexhaustible resources of God are made available to us.

Third, the expression of that love is worked out in daily living through discipline and character training. This is when the love that comes from God is made available to our fellow human beings through us.

The first time I saw Niagara Falls, I equated that tremendous quantity of water to the love of God being poured out. Then

I thought to myself, "Nevertheless, its real purpose is not fulfilled merely in the outpouring. Only when that power is channeled and used to bring light, heat, and power to the inhabitants of many of the major cities of the North American continent is the purpose achieved."

That is how it is with us. We receive God's love when we are born again; it is poured out over us by the Holy Spirit; but it only becomes available to our fellow human beings as it is channeled through our lives in discipline and training.

Chapter Ten

How to Open Up to the Holy Spirit

How can we open up to the Holy Spirit and receive Him in His fullness, and through Him receive all the blessings promised? We will look at a number of Scriptures which state the conditions we need to satisfy in order to receive the fullness of the Holy Spirit. God does require us to fulfill a number of specific essentials.

Repent and Be Baptized

Acts 2:37-38 is the end of Peter's talk on the day of Pentecost, and it gives the response of the people to his message:

37When the people heard this, they were cut to the heart and said to Peter and the other apostles, "Brothers, what shall we do?"

[That was a specific question, and God's Word gives a specific answer.]

38Peter replied, "Repent and be baptized, every one of you, in the name of Jesus Christ so that your sins may be forgiven. And you will receive the gift of the Holy Spirit." (NIV)

There we have the promise: *"You will receive the gift of the Holy Spirit."* We also have two conditions clearly stated: *"Repent and be baptized."* To repent means to turn sincerely from all sinfulness and rebellion and submit ourselves without reservation to God and to His requirements. To be baptized is to go through an ordinance or a sacrament by which each of us is personally and visibly identified with Jesus Christ to the world in His death, burial and resurrection. So there are two basic, primary requirements for receiving the gift of the Holy Spirit: we must repent, and we must be baptized.

Ask God

In Luke 11:9-13, Jesus says:

> [9]*"So I say to you: Ask and it will be given to you; seek and you will find; knock and the door will be opened to you.*
> [10]*For everyone who asks receives; he who seeks finds; and to him who knocks, the door will be opened.*
> [11]*Which of you fathers, if your son asks for a fish, will give him a snake instead?*
> [12]*Or if he asks for an egg, will give him a scorpion?*
> [13]*If you then, though you are evil, know how to give good gifts to your children, how much more will your Father in heaven give the Holy Spirit to those who ask him!"*
>
> *(NIV)*

Here is a simple condition but a very important one. Jesus says the Father will give the Holy Spirit to His children if we ask Him for the Holy Spirit. I have heard Christians say, "I don't need to ask for the Holy Spirit." I must tell you that is not scriptural. Jesus was speaking to His disciples and He said, "Your Father will give you the Holy Spirit *if you **ask** for it.*" Elsewhere Jesus said He would go to the Father and ask the Father to send the Holy Spirit to His disciples. My feeling is that if Jesus had to ask the Father, it will not do us any harm to ask as well. This, then, is the third condition: to ask.

Be Thirsty

In John 7:37-39, we have three more simple conditions stated:

> *37On the last and greatest day of the Feast, Jesus stood and said in a loud voice, "If a man is thirsty, let him come to me and drink.*
> *38Whoever believes in me, as the Scripture has said, streams of living water will flow from within him."*
> *39By this he meant the Spirit, whom those who believed in him were later to receive. Up to that time the Spirit had not been given, since Jesus had not yet been glorified.* (NIV)

The author of the gospel makes it very clear that in this passage Jesus was talking about believers receiving the Holy Spirit. With that in mind, let us look at what Jesus said. *"If a man is thirsty, let him come to me and drink."* These are three simple but practical requirements.

The first is we must be thirsty. God does not force His blessings on people who feel they do not need them. Many people never receive the fullness of the Holy Spirit because they are not really thirsty. If you think you have all you need already, why should God bother you with more? Very probably, you are not making the best use of what you already have. You would be under greater condemnation if God gave you more.

That is an essential condition—to be thirsty. To be thirsty means you have recognized you need more than you already have. As a matter of fact, thirst is one of the strongest desires in the human body.

When a person is really thirsty, they do not care about eating or anything else. All they want is a drink. I spent three years in deserts in North Africa, and I have a pretty good picture of what it means to be thirsty. When a man is thirsty, he does not bargain or talk or discuss; he just goes to where the water is. That is what Jesus was saying: you must be thirsty.

Come to Jesus

Then, if you are thirsty, He said, *"...come to me..."* So, the second condition is to come to Jesus. Jesus is the Baptizer in the Holy Spirit. If you want the baptism, you must come to the One who baptizes in the Holy Spirit. No human being baptizes in the Holy Spirit, only Jesus.

Drink

Then He said you must drink. This is so simple some people leave it out. But drinking is receiving something within you by a decision of your will and a physical response. It is also part of receiving the Holy Spirit. Thirsting, coming to Jesus, and drinking are all essential. Just being totally passive and saying, "Well, if God wants to do it, let Him do it!" is not drinking. Drinking is actively receiving within you.

Yield

We want to consider two more relevant facts concerning our physical bodies which were touched on in earlier sections. First, our bodies are destined by God to be the temples of the Holy Spirit. 1 Corinthians 6:19 says:

> [19]*Do you not know that your body is a temple of the Holy Spirit, who is in you, whom you have received from God?* (NIV)

Second, we are required to offer or yield to God the parts of our bodies as instruments for His service. This is our responsibility. Romans 6:13 states:

> [13]*Do not offer the parts of your body to sin, as instruments of wickedness, but rather offer yourselves to God, as those who have been brought from death to life; and offer the parts of your body to him [God] as instruments of righteousness.* (NIV)

We have a responsibility straight from the Scripture to offer, yield, or dedicate the various members of our physical bodies to God for His service. One member particularly needs God's control: the tongue. James says very simply in his epistle:

> [8]*...but no man can tame [or control] the tongue.* (James 3:8 NIV)

We need help from God to control all the members of our bodies, but we need special help with our tongues. When the Holy Spirit comes in in His fullness, the first member that He affects, takes control of, and utilizes for God's glory is the tongue. You will find, if you care to check, that every time the New Testament speaks of people being filled with the Holy Spirit or full of the Holy Spirit, the first immediate result is some utterance that comes out of their mouths. They speak, they prophesy, they praise, they sing, they speak in tongues—but always the mouth is engaged. When you come to Jesus and drink, the final result will be an overflow, and it will be out of your mouth. This principle is stated by Jesus very clearly in Matthew 12:34: *"For out of the overflow of the heart the mouth speaks."*

When your heart is filled to overflowing, the overflow will take place through your mouth in speech. God wants you not to have just enough, He wants you to have an overflow. Remember, He said, *"...out of his inner being will flow rivers of living water."* That is the ultimate purpose of God.

God's Requirements

The following are the seven conditions that I have found in the Bible for receiving the fullness of the Holy Spirit:

1. Repent.
2. Be baptized.
3. Ask God.
4. Be thirsty.
5. Come to Jesus; He's the baptizer.
6. Drink—receive within yourself.
7. Present your body as a temple for the Holy Spirit and your members as instruments of righteousness.

Perhaps you are left wondering how you can do all this. I want to help you by sharing a pattern prayer that includes the things I have been explaining to you. Read it over, and, if it is your prayer, pray it aloud to the Lord.

Lord Jesus, I'm thirsty for the fullness of Your Holy Spirit. I present my body to You as a temple and my members as instruments of righteousness, especially my tongue, the member I cannot tame. Fill me, I pray, and let Your Holy Spirit flow through my lips in rivers of praise and worship. Amen.

If you prayed that prayer sincerely, it has been heard, and the results are on the way. You may be quite surprised at the fullness of what you will receive.